Being a
Good Citizen

Joanna Ponto

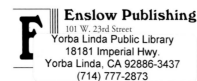

Enslow Publishing
101 W. 23rd Street

Published in 2016 by Enslow Publishing, LLC.
101 W. 23rd Street, Suite 240, New York, NY 10011

Library of Congress Cataloging-in-Publication Data
Ponto, Joanna.
 Being a good citizen / Joanna Ponto.
    pages cm. — (All about character)
 Includes bibliographical references and index.
 Summary: "Provides character education through different scenarios that demonstrate children being good citizens"—Provided by publisher.
ISBN 978-0-7660-7103-2 (library binding)
ISBN 978-0-7660-7101-8 (pbk.)
ISBN 978-0-7660-7102-5 (6-pack)
1. Citizenship—Juvenile literature. 2. Children—Conduct of life—Juvenile literature. I. Title.
JF801.P66 2016
323.6'5—dc23
                            2015000151

Printed in the United States of America

To Our Readers: We have done our best to make sure all Web sites in this book were active and appropriate when we went to press. However, the author and the publisher have no control over and assume no liability for the material available on those Web sites or on any Web sites they may link to. Any comments or suggestions can be sent by e-mail to customerservice@enslow.com.

Contents

Words to Know

citizen   helpful   volunteer

A person who is a good citizen cares about himself or herself and the community. A good citizen is helpful and follows rules.

5

Andre likes to play in the park with his friends. He asks other children to play with him too. Andre is a good citizen.

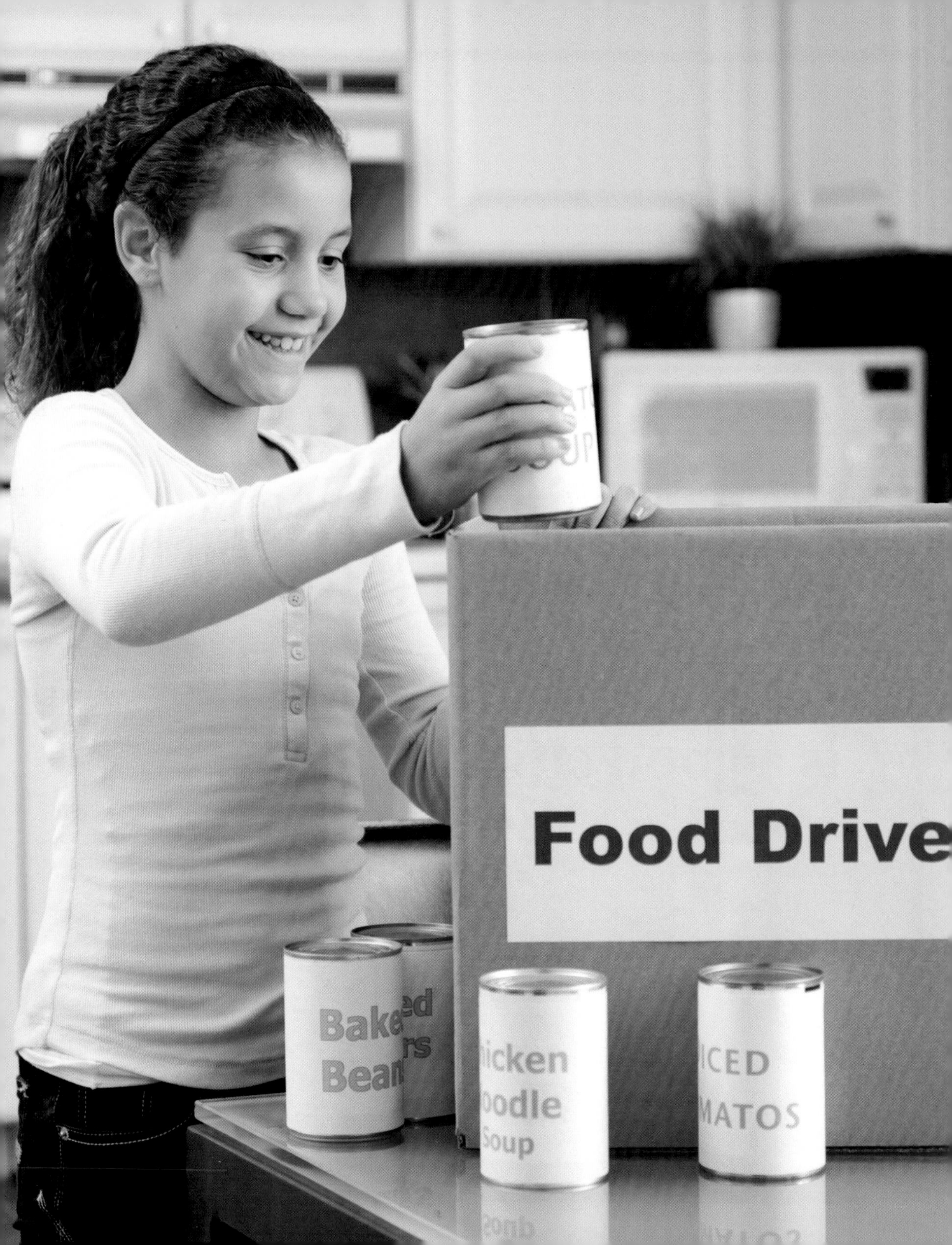
Food Drive

Rosa collects food for the poor. She brings it to a homeless shelter. Rosa is a good citizen.

Ken follows the rules. He puts on his seatbelt when he gets into a car. Ken is a good citizen.

Kate helps new kids at school. She shows them where their classes are. She asks them to sit at her lunch table. Kate is a good citizen.

John tried out for the school play. His friend got the part John wanted. John was happy for his friend. John is a good citizen.

Layla gets good grades in math. She helps her friend who has trouble with his math homework. Layla is a good citizen.

Amber volunteers at an animal shelter. She feeds and plays with animals that do not have homes. Amber is a good citizen.

Dan washes the dishes after dinner. He keeps his room clean. He helps shovel snow. Dan is a good citizen.

Erin carries groceries for her grandma. Her grandma cannot walk very well. Erin is a good citizen.

Read More

Hanson, Anders. *Do Something for Others: The Kids' Book of Citizenship.* Edina, Minn.: ABDO Publishing, 2014.

Hoffman, Mary Ann. *I Am a Good Citizen*. New York: Gareth Stevens, 2011.

Web Sites

Citizenship: Rights, Rules, and Responsibilities
studyzone.org/testprep/ss5/b/citizrrrl.cfm

Global Kids Connect: Being a Global Citizen
globalkidsconnect.org/global-citizen/

Index

Guided Reading Level: D
Guided Reading Leveling System is based on the guidelines recommended by Fountas and Pinnell.

Word Count: 218